Kidwelly Castle

John R. Kenyon BA, MCLIP, FSA, FRHistS

Introduction

The Arrival of the Normans

The Norman conquest of England was completed within a few years of the battle of Hastings (1066); in contrast, the Anglo-Norman subjugation of Wales was not accomplished finally until the reign of Edward I (1272–1307). Of these two and a half centuries of conquest, castles are perhaps the most striking feature, and Kidwelly ranks as one of the finest.

Wales on the eve of the Norman incursions was made up of a number of kingships, the most powerful of which were Deheubarth in the south-west, Gwynedd in the north, Powys in the Welsh midlands and Morgannwg in the south-east. There was little or no unity between these kingships, although there were times when one Welsh ruler rose to lead resistance against the Norman invaders, often with considerable success.

The death in battle in 1093 of Rhys ap Tewdwr, ruler of Deheubarth, enabled the Normans to establish a greater foothold, however tenuous, across much of south Wales, for the sons of Rhys were too young to provide effective opposition. In the east, the Normans began to consolidate their hold on lands in the Welsh kingdoms of Brycheiniog and Morgannwg, the two areas that were to become the great medieval lordships of Brecon and Glamorgan respectively. To the west, Normans from the earldom of Shrewsbury moved down through central Wales and established a number of strongholds, including Cardigan and Pembroke, in 1093. Two years later, by royal command the sheriff of Devon built a castle at Rhydygors on the Tywi estuary, near Carmarthen. These Norman advances, however, were not made solely by overland routes; the sea offered another means of access and the invaders soon occupied much of the coastal strip of south Wales.

Impressive though this advance was, the Norman control of their newly acquired territories was always under threat and wherever they settled initially a castle, usually of earth and timber, was built as a

strong point. It could serve as a base from which further military campaigns could be launched, as a centre of defence and, if necessary, as a place of retreat. Yet a castle's function was rarely exclusively military; it was also a focus for colonization — so that a small borough often grew up in its shadow — as well as a symbol of domination from where newly conquered lands, or lordships, could be administered.

Nevertheless, a castle did not always guarantee permanent security. In a series of Welsh counter-attacks in 1096, Pembroke alone withstood the Welsh onslaught; even Rhydygors was abandoned by its garrison. The somewhat isolated pockets of Norman power, with their long lines of communication, were not strong enough at first to resist concerted attacks by the Welsh.

However, early in the reign of the new king of England, Henry I (1100–35), Norman control was reasserted in south Wales, with royal authority centred at Carmarthen. Additional castles were constructed at this time, some of which were deliberately situated in coastal areas alongside navigable rivers to protect the important coastal route. These fortifications also had the advantage that they could be supplied from the sea should the Welsh cut off the landward approaches. Kidwelly was one such fortification. Neighbouring castles were similarly located at Loughor to the east and Llansteffan and Laugharne to the west.

A scene from the Bayeux Tapestry depicting the construction of a typical Norman earth-and-timber castle at Hastings in 1066 (Musée de la Tapisserie, Bayeux, France. With special authorization of the City of Bayeux).

Above: A silver penny of King Henry I (1100–35), who reasserted Norman control in south Wales. Additional castles were built, including Kidwelly, which was probably established by the king's powerful minister, Roger, bishop of Salisbury (d. 1139), sometime around 1106 (National Museum of Wales).

Opposite: Kidwelly Castle is perched on a prominent ridge above the river Gwendraeth, close to its confluence with the Bristol Channel. The strategic position of the castle ensured control of the nearby coastal waters, as well as the protection of a vital supply route in the event of a landward siege.

A History of the Castle

Bishop Roger was renowned as a patron of architecture especially in Wiltshire and Dorset, but he was also probably responsible for the first castle at Kidwelly. This twelfth-century monument attributed to Roger is in Salisbury Cathedral (Dean and Chapter, Salisbury Cathedral).

Right: Bishop Roger's sumptuous castle-palace at Sherborne (Old Castle) in Dorset (English Heritage: Skyscan Balloon Photography).

Far right: Roger was also responsible for two ambitious building projects at Old Sarum, Wiltshire: the castle's royal palace and the rebuilding of the old cathedral (English Heritage: Skyscan Balloon Photography).

Bishop Roger and the First Castle

In 1102, as a matter of political expediency, Henry I entrusted the Welsh territory (or commote) of Cydweli, along with Ystrad Tywi and Gower, to Hywel ap Goronwy, a Welshman who had risen to favour at a time when the king was threatened by the powerful Montgomery family. Once this threat had subsided and following Hywel's murder in 1106, Henry re-established Norman control by installing his trusted advisor, Roger, bishop of Salisbury (d. 1139), as lord of Kidwelly. The building of the castle and the town probably started soon after.

Roger was a remarkable man; he had been a priest in the town of Avranches in Normandy, before joining Prince Henry's household, where he served so successfully that he was quickly promoted to higher office when Henry became king. Serving as chancellor, bishop of Salisbury and as the king's chief minister, Roger became one of the most important figures in English politics in the early twelfth century, controlling the kingdom's administration and finances, sometimes for long periods when the king was absent.

Bishop Roger was also a prodigious builder and patron of architecture, and was remembered as such by his contemporaries: William of Malmesbury emphasized the tremendous personal pride that he took in his buildings. The finest example that survives is the bishop's own castle or fortified palace of Sherborne (Old Castle) in Dorset, which was built between about 1122 and 1137. Roger was also responsible for two ambitious projects at Old Sarum (Salisbury) in Wiltshire: the castle's royal palace and the rebuilding of the old cathedral, though now both are reduced to foundations. Even less survives of the magnificent castles that he built at Malmesbury and Devizes — the latter described by Henry of Huntingdon as 'the most splendid castle in Europe'.

The first mention of a castle at Kidwelly occurs in the foundation charter of the small Benedictine priory there — that other symbol of Norman colonization that accompanied castle and town — dated between 1107 and 1114. The priory was established as a daughter house of Sherborne Abbey in Dorset, and its charter was issued from the hall of Kidwelly Castle in the presence of a number of witnesses, including a certain Edmund, who

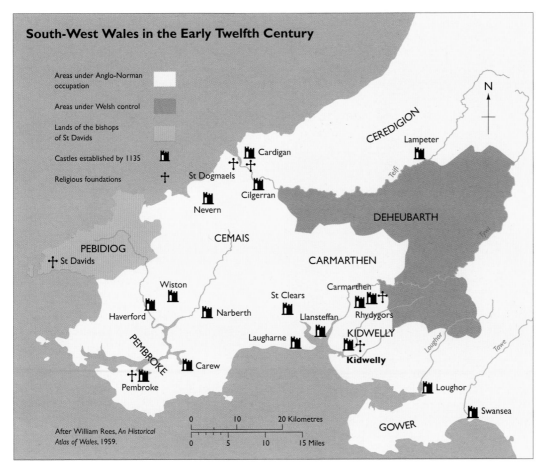

South-West Wales in the Early Twelfth Century

Areas under Anglo-Norman occupation

Areas under Welsh control

Lands of the bishops of St Davids

Castles established by 1135

Religious foundations

CEREDIGION

Lampeter

Cardigan

St Dogmaels

Cilgerran

Nevern

DEHEUBARTH

CEMAIS

CARMARTHEN

PEBIDIOG

St Davids

Carmarthen

Wiston

St Clears

Rhydygors

Narberth

Llansteffan

KIDWELLY

Haverford

Laugharne

Kidwelly

PEMBROKE

Carew

Loughor

Pembroke

Swansea

GOWER

After William Rees, *An Historical Atlas of Wales*, 1959.

0   10   20 Kilometres

0   5   10   15 Miles

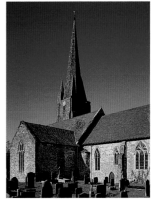

The foundation charter for a small Benedictine priory at Kidwelly was issued from the hall of the castle sometime between 1107 and 1114. Established as a daughter house of Sherborne Abbey, Dorset, part of the later priory church survives in use as the town's parish church.

had charge of the castle on behalf of Bishop Roger. The earliest fortification must have been built by this time, or was close to being completed. The newly erected defences would have provided a secure haven for immigrant settlers, as well as being a centre from which the recently created lordship could be administered.

The site for Kidwelly was well chosen: Bishop Roger was able to make use of natural defences to the east by building his castle on the side of a ridge above a steep scarp which runs down to the river Gwendraeth. To complete the enclosure, an earthen bank with a ditch in the shape of a crescent was constructed to form the defended perimeter away from the slope. Limited excavations undertaken in 1930 and 1931 against the later outer curtain confirmed that the original bank and ditch were Norman, but the construction of the later medieval castle may have removed all other traces of the twelfth-century stronghold.

This type of early castle, with an earthen bank and deep ditch enclosing a circular or partially circular area, is known as a ringwork, and would have had additional timber defences. Therefore, although no traces have been recovered at Kidwelly, it is likely that a timber palisade topped the rampart, perhaps with wooden towers projecting from it at intervals. The palisade would probably have continued along the edge of the scarp above the river, where a bank may have been thought unnecessary, perhaps with a timber gatehouse on the site of the existing south gatehouse, and possibly a further gate on the site of the present north gatehouse.

Nevertheless, even though the overall shape of Bishop Roger's castle heavily influenced its future development, we cannot be certain of the nature of the timber defences or the timber buildings inside the castle at this time. Moreover, a piece of carved Norman stonework (now mislaid) that was found reused inside the castle may indicate at least one

The earliest fortification at Kidwelly was built of earth and timber with enclosures to the north and south. These early earthen enclosures determined the development of the castle and town, the fossilized outline of which can be seen in this aerial view of Kidwelly (Royal Commission on the Ancient and Historical Monuments of Wales).

An artist's impression of how the earliest earth-and-timber stronghold at Kidwelly may have looked in the twelfth century. Apart from the ringwork bank, the form of the defences and the internal buildings are entirely conjectural (Illustration by Geraint Derbyshire, 1990).

substantial masonry structure — possibly the hall noted in the priory charter. So, it is not inconceivable that part of Kidwelly was built of stone from the beginning, especially when we consider what Bishop Roger achieved elsewhere.

Besides the hall, within the defences there would have been other domestic buildings, such as stables, a kitchen, accommodation, and perhaps a chapel. Traces of these may lie under the present surface, for at a later date the interior of the castle was levelled up by 2 to 7 feet (0.6-2m).

To the north and south of the castle were additional enclosures making a huge defended area. Originally, they may have been a single enclosure but a small Norman town soon occupied the southern part. The present layout of the town defences may well date from this time, though, like the castle, they would have been constructed of earth and timber. Known sometimes as the 'old town' — as opposed to the later medieval new town on the other side of the river, the two linked by a late medieval bridge — an early twelfth-century document indicates that the burgesses were drawn from French (Norman) and English (Anglo-Saxon) settlers, as well as Flemings.

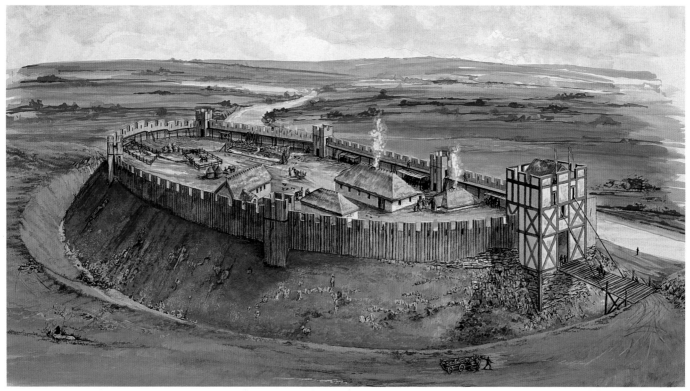

The outworks to the north further defended both town and castle; access to this area from Bishop Roger's castle may have been through a gate on the north side. In addition, the castle and the town defences could have had water-filled ditches or moats as part of the fortifications, the water being channelled down from the adjacent hills, as later records and place names suggest.

Maurice de Londres and the Welsh Capture of the Castle

Roger seems to have still held the castle in 1136, when mention is made of his constable, Geoffrey. However, Gerald of Wales (Giraldus Cambrensis) informs us that at about the same time Maurice de Londres (d. 1149) — whose father, William (d. about 1126), had established the castle of Ogmore and founded the church at neighbouring Ewenny (Glamorgan) — was in a position of

authority in the Kidwelly area. And it was in 1136 that Maurice defeated and killed Gwenllian — wife of Gruffudd ap Rhys, lord of Deheubarth (d. 1137) — in battle outside Kidwelly, as she sought to repulse a Norman counter-attack launched in her husband's absence. Maurice's campaign was in response to a notable Welsh victory near Loughor, which itself was an episode in a widespread uprising against Anglo-Norman rule in south Wales that took place in 1136–37.

Gwenllian and her two eldest sons, Morgan and Maelgwn, took to the field against Maurice in an initiative that later led Gerald of Wales to describe her 'like some second Penthesilea, Queen of the Amazons'. Both Gwenllian and Morgan were slain, and Maelgwn was taken prisoner at the site, which is still known as Maes Gwenllian (Gwenllian's Field), just a short distance from the castle.

Three years later, in 1139, Bishop Roger fell from the favour of the new king, Stephen (1135–54), who deprived him of his lands. Both the castle and the lordship of Kidwelly must have passed to Maurice de Londres at that time, if not earlier. Although his heirs held the castle thereafter more or less continuously

In 1136 Maurice de Londres (d. 1149) defeated and killed the Welsh princess, Gwenllian, in battle at Kidwelly; by 1139 the castle and lordship were in his hands. Maurice's handsome tomb slab lies in the church founded by his father at Ewenny, Glamorgan.

The Princes of Deheubarth

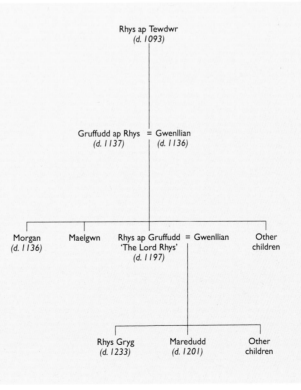

Rhys ap Tewdwr
(d. 1093)

Gruffudd ap Rhys = Gwenllian
(d. 1137)   (d. 1136)

Morgan | Maelgwn | Rhys ap Gruffudd = Gwenllian | Other
(d. 1136) | | 'The Lord Rhys' | children
| | (d. 1197) |

Rhys Gryg | Maredudd | Other
(d. 1233) | (d. 1201) | children

A Welsh prince from a mid-thirteenth-century copy of the great Welsh law book of Hywel Dda (National Library of Wales, Peniarth Ms. 28, f. 1v).

Left: Gwenllian, wife of Gruffudd ap Rhys, and mother of the Lord Rhys, was 'like some second Penthesilea' — according to Gerald of Wales. This memorial to Gwenllian lies just outside the main gate of the castle.

Right: The Lord Rhys (d. 1197) — to whom this fourteenth-century tomb effigy in St Davids Cathedral is attributed — was a ruler of outstanding ability and he is known to have built or refurbished a number of castles.

Far right: Although Brut y Tywysogyon (Chronicle of the Princes) *records that Rhys 'built the castle of Cydweli' in 1190 following the Welsh capture of the fortress, the extent of his work here is not known (National Library of Wales, Peniarth Ms. 20, p. 196).*

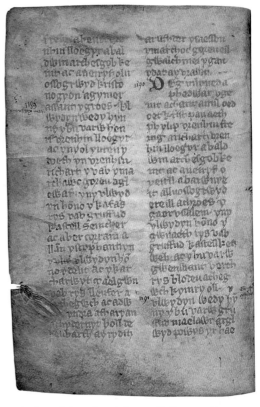

A thirteenth-century silvered bronze ring brooch from Kidwelly (National Museum of Wales).

until 1216, there were times in the twelfth and thirteenth centuries when castle and town were lost to the Welsh for short periods.

The capture of a castle was not an inconsiderable achievement, and in 1159 Rhys ap Gruffudd (d. 1197), prince of Deheubarth, is recorded as having captured and burnt those castles that the Normans had built in south-west Wales, and Kidwelly may well have been one of them.

The Lord Rhys, as he was later known, was the youngest son of Gwenllian and Gruffudd ap Rhys, and was only four years old at the time of his mother's death in 1136. Rhys was to become a ruler of outstanding ability in medieval Wales and he dominated politics in the south-west in the later twelfth century. This was achieved to some extent with the consent of King Henry II (1154–89) after Rhys had accepted client status in an agreement sealed during negotiations between the two rulers at nearby Laugharne and Pembroke in 1171–72.

Rhys is known to have built or refurbished a number of castles, including Cardigan (1171) and perhaps Dinefwr, the ancient seat of the kingdom of Deheubarth. In 1190, a year after the death of Henry II

and when diplomatic relations with the new king, Richard I (1189–99), had soured, Rhys went on the offensive and the Welsh chronicles record that he 'built the castle of Cydweli'. Although we have no idea what this entailed — it may simply have been major repairs to what was presumably still an earth-and-timber castle — Rhys's reputation as a builder of castles could mean that his building at Kidwelly involved masonry work. Whatever Rhys had achieved at Kidwelly, the castle was back in Anglo-Norman hands by 1201, for his death in 1197 had led to internal conflict and a struggle for power amongst the Welsh of Deheubarth.

The early thirteenth century witnessed the rise of the house of Gwynedd under the masterly guidance of Llywelyn ab Iorwerth (Llywelyn the Great; d. 1240), at the expense of Deheubarth. Llywelyn succeeded in uniting much of Wales against the Anglo-Normans and it was during his successful campaign in 1215 that he sanctioned Rhys Gryg (d. 1233), the eldest son of the Lord Rhys, to capture and burn Kidwelly. It was not until 1220 that Rhys reluctantly relinquished the castle to the heiress to Kidwelly, Hawise de Londres (d. 1274), at the behest of the prince of Gwynedd.

If references to what the Normans undertook at Kidwelly are tantalizingly sparse, we are faced with a similar situation regarding those periods when the castle was in Welsh hands. Recent re-examination of the outer curtain wall of the castle has revealed that the lower third of the inner face of the section between towers 2 and 3 (p. 34) is earlier than the rest of the curtain. In the light of comparison with the development of the earliest stone defences at the neighbouring castles of Laugharne and Llansteffan, it seems likely that this stretch of wall represents Kidwelly's first stone defences, dating to the late twelfth or early thirteenth century. Unfortunately, we cannot be certain who was responsible for building this curtain wall. Perhaps it was part of the Lord Rhys's work of 1190; alternatively it could have been repair work necessary either after the Anglo-Norman recovery of Kidwelly in 1201, or possibly after the Welsh had surrendered the castle once again in 1220.

Payn and Patrick de Chaworth: A Military Stronghold

Hawise de Londres took as her first husband Walter de Braose, who was killed during the Welsh war of 1233–34. Before this, Kidwelly had been attacked again and destroyed or badly damaged during Llywelyn's southern campaign of 1231. In 1243, Maredudd (d. 1271), son of Rhys Gryg, surrendered the lordship of Kidwelly into the hands of Hawise and her third husband, Patrick de Chaworth, for which they had to pay one hundred marks to the Crown. In 1258, Patrick fell fighting the Welsh, and, although the town of Kidwelly was burnt in this campaign, the castle was strong enough to hold out.

Hawise had two sons by her third marriage, Payn (d. 1279) and Patrick (d. 1283), who inherited Kidwelly successively following their mother's death in 1274. Although Payn died young, by the time of his death he was one of the more powerful lords of the Welsh March, enjoying considerable authority in south Wales. He had accompanied the Lord Edward (later King Edward I, 1272–1307) on crusade between 1270 and 1274, and he had served as one of the king's commanders in the 1277 war against the powerful prince of Wales, Llywelyn ap Gruffudd (d. 1282), grandson of Llywelyn ab Iorwerth.

Little documentary evidence survives for new construction work at Kidwelly, but it was at this time that much of the castle that survives today was begun. Building is not likely to have started until at least 1275, after Payn had returned from crusade. A clue to this work takes the form of receipts for loans of £40 and £320 from King Edward in March 1277, for 'his own use', which could have included the refortification of the castle.

Of the castle itself, we know that the outer curtain already existed in stone (above). The first phase of the Chaworth works therefore almost certainly concentrated on the inner ward in order to bring Kidwelly up to date with the sophisticated defensive/offensive requirements of a modern military stronghold.

The inner ward at Kidwelly was built with four great round towers linked by curtain walls, from which archers on the battlements could fire into the field of attack and flank the adjacent stretches of curtain wall to prevent it being scaled. This design is reminiscent of other castles of the period, including Conwy, built by Edward I in the 1280s, and Caerphilly, begun in 1268 by the powerful earl of Gloucester and lord of Glamorgan, Gilbert de Clare (d. 1295), both of whom the Chaworths would have known.

Payn (d. 1279) and Patrick de Chaworth (d. 1283) held Kidwelly successively between 1274 and 1283, during which time the castle was strengthened and brought up to date militarily. The seal of Patrick appears on this manuscript dated 1281 (The National Archives: PRO, DL 27/57).

Conwy Castle, built by King Edward I (1272–1307) between 1283 and 1287, was designed with a powerful inner ward — a pattern repeated elsewhere in Wales, including Kidwelly, which soon became an equally formidable stronghold.

From the outset, the south-east tower appears to have been built higher than its three companions, perhaps to serve as the principal accommodation for the lords of Kidwelly. Unlike its counterparts, there are no signs of blocked battlements that mark the heightening of the other three towers in the fourteenth century; it also boasts a greater degree of comfort, having three fireplaces compared with the more meagre provision elsewhere. Such an arrangement, where a principal round tower dominates an inner enclosure, is not unusual — for example at Edward I's castle at Flint (begun 1277).

The rather awkward manner in which the towers were squeezed into the existing enclosure is evident from the plan. The north and south gateways are relatively simple affairs, merely defended passages through the curtain, but flanked, of course, by the inner ward towers. Little is known of the buildings inside the inner ward, though there was probably a hall, which may have been on the site of the existing building.

With the inner ward well under way, if not already complete, the Chaworths turned their attention to the outer curtain wall. Apart from the section described earlier (p. 9), the curtain was rebuilt with four mural towers, the north gatehouse, and presumably the original south gate. The surviving walling of this period runs from tower 1, via the north gate and the now collapsed tower 4, to the north-east tower of the inner ward. Originally, the backs of the mural towers probably had timber-framed and plastered rear walls.

With the inner and outer curtains now complete, Kidwelly had become a truly concentric castle. It had one defensive circuit within another — with the towers of the inner ward overlooking the outer curtain — so that archers on both sets of walls could fire at an attacking force simultaneously. In theory at least, this doubled the firepower of the castle, assuming that it had the garrison to man all the defences.

Unfortunately, we do not know what the south gate looked like at this time, for the present structure was begun in the late fourteenth century and removed all trace of any earlier building. Nevertheless, a strong gatehouse would have been vital to protect the most vulnerable part of the castle — the entrance — as well as to provide accommodation of a quality to match the status of great lords like the Chaworths, or the constable of the castle. Elsewhere, gatehouses became increasingly sophisticated during the thirteenth century and were frequently equipped with a series of obstacles to thwart attackers, including towers equipped with arrowslits flanking a gate-passage, murder holes, portcullises and strong doors.

By the 1280s Kidwelly had been transformed into a military stronghold on a par with the other great castles built in Wales during the late thirteenth century, including the royal castles in the north and Caerphilly in Glamorgan. It was certainly strong enough to serve as a storehouse for the king's money on its way to Carmarthen in 1283, and comfortable enough for the monarch to spend several days there a year later. Nor were the town defences neglected; funding was granted for rebuilding them in masonry in the 1280s, though the south gate was not completed until about 1300.

Rarely do we get a glimpse of what domestic life was like in a castle, but an inventory taken on the death of Patrick de Chaworth records his effects in the castle and lordship. Besides cattle, stud mares, wagons and carts, the inventory lists four tables with trestles in the castle's hall, together with five benches, and various barrels, copper vessels, cooking pots, and a salt cellar. Although this may seem meagre to us today, such a list is not unexpected given that any great lord would have travelled between his various residences taking with him his household trappings, including such items as wall hangings, table linen, silverware and even a bed. All of these items would have created a lavish display in the otherwise relatively empty shell of a castle and would have reinforced the status of the lord.

A cooking pot from Kidwelly, about 1300 (National Museum of Wales).

Opposite: By the end of the thirteenth century, Kidwelly Castle was a sophisticated stronghold with concentric — walls within walls — defences. This aerial view of the castle shows how soldiers on top of the inner ward towers could defend the outer ward or fire over the lower outer curtain wall (Crown Copyright).

Below: An early fourteenth-century manuscript illustration from the Luttrell Psalter *showing diners at a trestle table; four such tables were recorded in the hall at Kidwelly on the death of Patrick de Chaworth in 1283 (British Library, Additional Ms. 42130, f. 208r).*

Right: The magnificent tomb effigy of William de Valence in Westminster Abbey. William was granted Kidwelly in 1283 by Edward I to offset a debt and he appears to have held the castle until his death in 1296 (Dean and Chapter of Westminster).

Far right: Kidwelly passed to the house of Lancaster at the end of the thirteenth century and in 1333 was granted to Henry (d. 1361), later first duke of Lancaster. During this period, domestic comforts appear to have been as important as military considerations. This fifteenth-century manuscript illustration of Duke Henry is from the Bruges Garter Book (British Library, Stowe Ms. 594, f. 8).

This early fourteenth-century wine jug may have been imported directly to Kidwelly from south-west France (National Museum of Wales).

William de Valence and Henry of Lancaster: The Castle Made Comfortable

When Patrick de Chaworth died in 1283, his infant daughter, Matilda (Maud), was just one year old and too young to inherit Kidwelly. Instead, King Edward granted the castle to his uncle, William de Valence, lord of Pembroke (1247–96) in December 1283. Edward was in debt to his uncle for a sum of over £1,000, and, although William himself owed a smaller amount to the king, the Crown granted Kidwelly and its lordship to William in order to offset the debt.

By this time, it seems that William de Valence had already undertaken considerable improvements to his castles at Pembroke — including a sumptuous new suite of domestic buildings — and Goodrich in Herefordshire. He was therefore entirely capable of continuing the Chaworth reconstruction of Kidwelly, which he appears to have held until his death in 1296.

On his death, however, Kidwelly reverted to the Chaworth heiress, Matilda (Maud), who in 1291 had been granted in marriage by Edward I to his nephew, Henry (d. 1345), the second son of the king's brother, Edmund 'Crouchback', earl of Lancaster (1267–96). Henry was only about ten years old at this time, and the actual marriage ceremony did not take place until 1298. Henry succeeded his brother as earl of Lancaster in 1327, and in 1333 he bestowed Kidwelly — as well as his other Welsh estates — on his son, Henry, who styled himself 'lord of Kidwelly' until he succeeded his father in 1345. Henry died without a male heir in 1361 and a year later the castle was eventually settled on his daughter, Blanche (d. 1369), the wife of John of Gaunt, who later became duke of Lancaster (1362–99). On the succession of their son, Henry, in 1399 as the first Lancastrian king of England (Henry IV, 1399–1413), Kidwelly passed into the hands of the Crown.

Although architectural evidence indicates otherwise, there is no surviving documentary evidence for building work between the time the castle was granted to William de Valence in 1283 and when it passed to John of Gaunt in 1362. Much of the new building work nevertheless appears to date from the last twenty years of the thirteenth century and could therefore have been started by the Chaworths or William de Valence or Henry of Lancaster and continued by subsequent owners.

A large hall and solar (a lord's private chamber) were built above undercrofts to run the length of the east side of the inner ward, making use of the late thirteenth-century curtain on the east side at basement level. This new range connected the existing chambers in the south-east and north-east towers, and may have replaced a smaller hall block built by the Chaworths. As the focus for formal occasions in the castle, the hall would have been a prestigious building, equipped to receive guests, administer justice and reflect the status of the lord of Kidwelly. The construction of a well-appointed solar also suggests that domestic considerations were becoming increasingly important. During the relatively peaceful years that followed the Edwardian conquest, the accommodation in the south-east tower would have been cramped and unsuitable as the main residence in the castle. It was relegated to use by the lord's household and by the later Middle Ages it is referred to increasingly as the Exchequer Tower.

Soon after the completion of this range, a chapel was built at the southern end of the hall in a tower projecting down the slope towards the river. This presumably replaced an earlier chapel, the location of which is unknown. The chapel itself, on the top floor of the tower, has particularly fine windows — similar to those of the solar — and the architectural style of the building, with deeply splayed spur buttresses, suggests that it dates from the very end of the thirteenth century (p. 43).

Medieval documents sometimes refer to the chapel as the 'king's chantry'; a chantry is a chapel that has been endowed for the saying of Mass for the soul of a particular person, often the founder of the chapel. From contemporary accounts, we learn that one Thomas Davy, chaplain, was paid an annual salary of 74s. 4d. in 1369–70 'to find bread, wine and candles both for himself and for a certain monk to celebrate within the chapel' — a practice which

The Descent of Kidwelly Castle in the Thirteenth and Fourteenth Centuries

(1) Walter de Braose = Hawise de Londres = (3) Patrick de Chaworth
(d. about 1233–34) (d. 1274) (d. 1258)

(2) Henry de Turberville
(d. between 1234–39)

Henry III
(1216–72)

Payn de Chaworth
(d. 1279)

Patrick de Chaworth
(d. 1283)

Edmund 'Crouchback'
[Earl of Lancaster]
(1267–96)

Edward I
(1272–1307)

Maud =
Henry
[Earl of Lancaster]
(1327–45)

Thomas
[Earl of Lancaster]
(1298–1322)

Edward II
(1307–27)

Henry
[Earl of Lancaster/Duke of Lancaster]
(1345–51)   (1351–61)

Edward III
(1327–77)

Maud
(d. 1362)

Blanche =
(d. 1369)

John of Gaunt
[Duke of Lancaster]
(1362–99)

Henry IV
(1399–1413)

Mid-fourteenth-century accounts record that a chaplain and monk were paid to celebrate Mass in the castle chapel. This almost contemporary manuscript illustration shows a priest raising the Host during Mass, watched by members of the Butler family of Wem, Shropshire, in their private chapel (Walters Art Gallery, Baltimore, Ms. W 105, f. 15).

continued for at least another hundred years. And in 1381–82 a large candle was bought for the chapel, weighing 8lbs and costing 5s. 10d., 'for the elevation of the Host' or bread, during the prayer of consecration in the Mass. Although we cannot be certain of the founder, or whose soul was being remembered in this way, one possible candidate is Henry of Lancaster, who retired from public life in 1333 to devote himself to religious contemplation until his death in 1345.

Across the inner ward from the hall, in the south-west corner, lies the kitchen block and a latrine, which is thought to be part of the late thirteenth-century remodelling.

John of Gaunt, shown in this late fourteenth-century manuscript illustration, held Kidwelly from 1362 until his death in 1399, during which time records indicate that work began on the construction of a grand new gatehouse (British Library, Cotton Nero Ms. D VII, f. 7).

Despite the emphasis on new domestic buildings, the defences were not ignored. The tops of the outer ward towers and the curtain walls between them were raised, supported on a prominent corbel table, mainly of red sandstone. At the same time, the mural towers were enclosed with masonry rear walls. As part of this work — or possibly as a result of it — the north-east and two western towers of the inner ward were raised a further stage. The new battlements on the two western towers were supported on corbels at a height to ensure a clear field of vision and fire across the newly raised outer curtain. The original Chaworth battlements or crenellations remain 'fossilized' within the late thirteenth-century masonry (p. 36).

It was probably at this time that the small defensive screen or mantlet wall was built, running north from the chapel tower to the north-east tower of the inner ward, although only a small section remains.

The Duchy of Lancaster: Administrative Centre

In the later Middle Ages, Kidwelly became more important as an administrative centre than as a residence for representatives of the Duchy of Lancaster. It was here that payments were collected from tenants for dispatch to London and justice was administered. As a result, remarkably detailed accounts survive for a period of almost two centuries and provide tantalizing glimpses of building operations and routine maintenance designed to ensure that the castle was fit to receive officials on Duchy business.

Although the recent building works already described (p. 13) were impressive, they were to be dwarfed by the improvements to the castle's main entrance, for it must have been decided that the centre of the Duchy's estates needed a more formidable symbol of its authority. The earlier entrance, presumably built by the Chaworths (p. 11), was for whatever reason no longer suitable, and Kidwelly's imposing new gate was to become one of the last great gatehouses to be built in England and Wales during the Middle Ages.

The first surviving record of work at Kidwelly, during John of Gaunt's tenure of the castle, dates

The Lordship of Kidwelly and the Duchy of Lancaster

When Bishop Roger re-established Norman control in the Kidwelly area in 1106, he did so by creating a lordship from the three native Welsh administrative units — or commotes — of Cydweli, Carnwyllion and Iscennen. Within what had been the commote of Cydweli, Norman, Flemish and English entrepreneurs were soon encouraged to settle in and around the burgeoning castle and town of Kidwelly as part of a wider immigration process that encompassed much of south-west Wales. Consequently, Kidwelly soon developed into a thriving burghal and commercial centre. Welshmen, on the other hand, were notable by their absence here as from almost all Anglo-Norman boroughs and as a result the area immediately surrounding Kidwelly came to be known as the Englishry or foreignry. But within three or four miles of the borough, the rest of the lordship remained thoroughly Welsh in character — as demonstrated by the number of Welsh names that appear in later building accounts (p. 17).

Although large tracts of the lordship lay under great forests, the low-lying areas of the Englishry possessed tracts of good pasture, which even in the early twelfth century were exploited for sheep grazing. These rich grasslands were of sufficient note to be recalled by Gerald of Wales when he described Maurice de Londres's 'broad pasture-lands, where he grazed a great flock of sheep'. No doubt this was the origin of the flourishing wool trade that sustained the fortunes of many of Kidwelly's burgesses throughout the Middle Ages. Significant, too, was Kidwelly's coastal location, which assured important trading links throughout south Wales, Bristol and as far afield as Ireland and Gascony.

In 1298, after a succession of Anglo-Norman lords, Kidwelly passed into the hands of the Lancaster family. They soon became absentee landlords who utilized the castle as a centre from which to administer the lordship, a process that gathered impetus when the lordship became part of the Duchy of Lancaster (p. 12). The castle's military and domestic roles were reduced further as farms, forests and mills were exploited for cash, rather than subsistence, to feed Duchy coffers. In 1399, with the accession of Henry IV, the Duchy passed into the hands of the reigning monarch, not in his role as king but as duke of Lancaster; and to this day it is administered on behalf of the sovereign by the Chancellor of the Duchy.

The Duchy of Lancaster owned considerable lands in England and Wales from which it derived a substantial income as well as considerable power. Divided into two 'parts' — north and south — Kidwelly, together with Ogmore, Grosmont, Skenfrith, White Castle, Monmouth, Brecon and Caldicot in Wales, came within the jurisdiction of the southern part. There was a whole bureaucracy to oversee the administration of revenues, legal proceedings, buildings and other matters. Locally at Kidwelly, the steward was the chief administrator and the receiver looked after the accounts, but the Duchy's auditor would visit the castle at least once a year to survey the administration and to see that there was no irregularity in the running of Duchy affairs. There were also visits by officers of the Duchy's council — as regular accounts record (pp. 17, 21). Kidwelly thus became a centre of administration and justice for the Lancaster estates in south-west Wales and, although the castle served but occasionally as a residence, Duchy officials continued to maintain the buildings for more than 250 years.

A mid-fourteenth-century seal of Henry of Lancaster (The National Archives: PRO, DL 27/192).

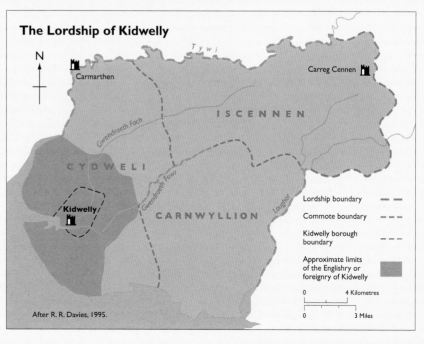

The Lordship of Kidwelly

N

Carmarthen

Carreg Cennen

Tywi

ISCENNEN

Gwendraeth Fach

CYDWELI

Gwendraeth Fawr

Kidwelly

CARNWYLLION

Loughor

Lordship boundary — —
Commote boundary – – –
Kidwelly borough boundary – – –
Approximate limits of the Englishry or foreignry of Kidwelly

0   4 Kilometres

0   3 Miles

After R. R. Davies, 1995.

*King Richard II (1377–99)
stayed at Kidwelly Castle
briefly in May 1399 on his
way to Ireland, following the
confiscation of Lancastrian
lands — including Kidwelly —
after the death of John of Gaunt.
The new gatehouse had probably
reached a significant height
by this time (Dean and Chapter
of Westminster).*

from around 1372. In that year he instructed Duchy officials to exempt from jury service his carpenter, John Nikel, and his mason, David Aleyn, on account of their being 'continually engaged in works' at Kidwelly. Later, in the reign of Richard II (1377–99), it appears that John of Gaunt decided to rebuild totally the castle's south gate — work that was to involve the complete removal of its predecessor — though he was not to live to see it finished. Records for 1388–89 mention the purchase of a quarry 'for the work of the new tower', as well as 9,000 shingles (wooden tiles) being made for roofing, and it would seem that this 'new tower' is the great gate that stands today. In 1395–96 more than £40 was spent on 'the new work of the Tower over the gates of the castle of Kidwelly'.

Matters became complicated in 1399, first with the death in February of John of Gaunt and the confiscation of the Lancastrian estates, including Kidwelly, which was granted to John Holland, duke of Exeter. Next came the political crisis that led to the overthrow of Richard II in September and the accession of Henry Bolingbroke, heir to Kidwelly, as king of England. Before this, however, Richard had stayed at Kidwelly for a night in May 1399 en route

to campaign in Ireland, and an account written after his deposition records the purchase of rushes for the floors for 1s. and wood worth 4s. for the fires.

The receiver's account for the same period, also compiled in hindsight, records an order to wall up the Kidwelly gate 'with stone and cement for its better defence to resist the malice of the former King Richard'. And, at about the same time, costs were incurred for 'carrying in the great old gates of the castle and removing them to the kitchen', at a cost of 5d., where they seem to have been cut up for firewood. There is also payment of 4d. for 'carrying the old castle gates into the castle', which may refer to a smaller set of gates.

By 1399, however, the new gatehouse appears to have reached a significant height, and would have acted as a considerable barrier. Therefore it seems unlikely that the blocking of the gate and the removal of the large wooden doors relate to John of Gaunt's gatehouse. It may be that the 'great old gates' belonged to the original gatehouse and had been left lying outside the castle. The other gates may have come from the north gatehouse, and early twentieth-century photographs do indeed show a wall added to the back of this gate, though unfortunately it is of unknown date.

*The coronation of Henry
Bolingbroke — the Lancastrian
heir to Kidwelly — as King Henry
IV (1399–1413). Work continued
on the gatehouse and must have
been close to completion in 1402
when the king ordered it to be
roofed in lead (British Library,
Harleian Ms. 4380, f. 186v).*

On a more domestic note, the same account describes the purchase of white linen cloth for boardcloths (tablecloths) and sanaps for use when the lord's officials were in residence — a reminder that table coverings were indicators of status. A sanap — another cloth used in conjunction with a boardcloth — was a mark of particular distinction and reserved for special occasions.

With the new king, Henry IV (1399–1413), installed, building work seems to have continued and accounts from 1400–01 demonstrate that work was still in progress on the 'construction and building of the said New gate and two towers and other diverse chambers in the said towers'. But payments were also recorded for the wages of six men for 'resisting the malice of Owain Glyn Dŵr'. Although the Glyn Dŵr rebellion broke out in 1400, Kidwelly does not seem to have been seriously threatened until the summer of 1403. Nevertheless, the new work must have taken on greater urgency for in February 1402 the king wrote to his official, William Langton, at Kidwelly and instructed that the gatehouse be completed and the roof covered with lead.

Remarkably, William Langton's account book for the works carried out at Kidwelly between April and October 1402 has survived. He recorded expenditure of over £100 on the gatehouse, with a workforce of more than seventy men — many of them Welshmen — consisting of quarrymen, masons (under the supervision of John Herde), labourers and carpenters, besides a number of men responsible for the carriage of materials. In the final month, preparations were made to protect the masonry from the winter's rain and frost by covering it with wood and straw. By the end of 1402, the new gate must have been almost complete for the following accounts indicate that the gatehouse was being fitted out with new locks for the prison doors and chains for prisoners.

Building and repair works, however, were not confined to the great gate; some considerable effort was spent on buildings elsewhere in the castle. Reference is made to repairs to the 'east' gate — perhaps the north gate — and the granary; a gutter was built 'from the door of the cellar to the door of the kitchen'; cribs and mangers were made for the stables and new furniture for the courthouse. Payment was made for 'cleansing the hall, chambers and courtyards between the gates' of the castle, and

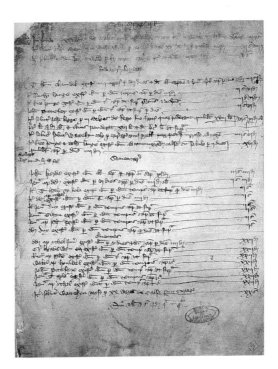

The 1402 account of William Langton furnishes detailed information on the expenditure on the new gatehouse in that year (The National Archives: PRO, DL 41/341).

the vestments and altar cloths from the chapel were washed as part of an ongoing programme of annual maintenance. Such matters were essential whilst Kidwelly played a major role in the administration of the Duchy of Lancaster: a role that we are reminded of by the purchase for 2*d.* of 'a bag bought from Wadyn Hobbe for books (for putting the session rolls in) when the Council was there'.

Siege and Rebuild

Elsewhere in Wales, the Glyn Dŵr rebellion had gathered pace and in the summer of 1403 news reached Kidwelly that a great offensive was being planned in south Wales. Hastily, seven archers and fourteen burgesses were assembled to defend the castle. The assault came in August, when a prominent member of the local Welsh gentry, Henry Don (d. 1416), an experienced soldier and former steward of Kidwelly, launched an attack on the castle. Although the town fell and several burgesses were killed, including Jenkin and Michael Don, the castle held firm during what came to be remembered as a long siege, which continued into October when the assault was renewed. By this time many of the townsfolk had fled east, some even to England if we are to believe the

An early fifteenth-century bronze belt fitting, with a figure of St Christopher, from Kidwelly (National Museum of Wales).

An artist's impression of how the town and castle of Kidwelly may have appeared in the 1403 siege. Temporary wooden defences might have protected the castle ditch and the barbican area in front of the gatehouse (Illustration by Ivan Lapper, 2002).

A fifteenth-century cannon from Cardiff Castle of the type that may have been sent as relief to Kidwelly (Cardiff County Council).

constable of the castle who so wrote to the king, whilst the remainder had fled into the castle. The siege was lifted, however, when the Welsh withdrew before winter set in.

Conditions inside the castle must have been grim. The garrison during this period of unrest (1403–06) was never very large, usually numbering about nine soldiers, but sometimes as many as twenty-one. It was supplemented by the town's burgesses, whom the Crown had stipulated must be born as Englishmen. The enlarged population may have placed a strain on provisions and it is not known whether quantities of wheat, oats, fish, wine and ale ordered for the castle's garrison in the September before the siege arrived in time. A cow, salt and wax, however, were purchased for 'provisioning of the castle during the siege this year'. Relief came in the way of additional arms: bows, two cannon, gunpowder and other munitions were sent from

London via the port of Bristol. Indeed, records indicate that £43 14s. 7d. was spent on arms for Kidwelly during 1403–04. There were more scares in the period 1403–06, including a further attack in the summer of 1404, when the town was again burnt.

The continuing seriousness of the situation is shown in the Duchy accounts of expenditure for the period, which seem to have been written with hindsight. Not surprisingly, works on the castle were minimal between 1403 and 1407, and were restricted to 'building work and repair … to fortify the said castle where it was most necessary'. Between 1403 and 1404, a new ditch was dug outside the north gate 'for the secure defence and safe keeping' of the castle against a number of Welsh rebels still encamped to the north. This bank and ditch are still visible, dividing the northern bailey into two unequal areas. In the same year, loops were made in palisades, and several roofs were repaired, including

Owain Glyn Dŵr

Owain was born about 1359 and could claim princely ancestry through both his parents. Educated at the law schools in London, he progressed from legal student to squire and soldier, serving in campaigns in Scotland and elsewhere. However, by 1400 he was comfortably established as a much-respected Welsh country gentleman, with residences at both Sycharth and Glyndyfrdwy. Wales, however, was unsettled at this time. Rising discontent, initially as a result of local land disputes induced by the overthrow of Richard II (1377–99), led some members of the gentry to contemplate rebellion, and in September 1400 Owain was proclaimed prince of Wales.

The Welsh, who were particularly skilled in the art of guerrilla warfare, as the English had often found to their cost, achieved some notable successes in the early years of the revolt. They won the battle of Bryn Glas, near Pilleth, Powys, in 1402; inflicted considerable damage on many towns, including Cardiff; and took some of the strongest castles in Wales, most notably Aberystwyth and Harlech.

In the summer of 1403 — the fourth year of the revolt — Owain Glyn Dŵr made a personal appearance in the Tywi valley, leading a strong force that captured a number of castles, including Dryslwyn and Carmarthen. It would seem that it was Owain's success that persuaded Henry Don, a former steward of the Duchy of Lancaster in the Kidwelly lordship and a man of considerable local power and standing — who was also ambitious and avaricious — to throw in his lot with the rebels. There is, however, no evidence that Owain himself was involved in the attack on Kidwelly town and castle; this was left to Henry Don himself.

However, even with French and Breton military support the tide began to turn around 1405, following an English victory at Usk. With the recapture of Aberystwyth and Harlech by the Crown between 1408 and 1409, the revolt was almost at an end. Owain himself rapidly faded from the annals, and by 1416 was probably dead.

Despite the Don family's role in the uprising, some members regained positions of authority in Kidwelly and elsewhere. Gruffudd Don, who accompanied his grandfather at the siege, was pardoned in 1413, as was Henry Don himself after terms of imprisonment in Kidwelly and Gloucester. Gruffudd was both constable of Kidwelly Castle and deputy-constable of Carmarthen Castle for a time, as well as receiver of Kidwelly for the Duchy of Lancaster. He also served with Henry V (1413-22) at the battle of Agincourt (1415), and in later campaigns in France during the Hundred Years War.

A gilt-bronze harness mount, bearing the arms of Owain Glyn Dŵr. It was found at Harlech Castle, which was successfully besieged by Glyn Dŵr in 1404 and held until 1409 (National Museum of Wales).

Above: Kidwelly Castle was besieged in 1403 by a Welsh force led by Henry Don in support of Owain Glyn Dŵr. This fifteenth-century Flemish manuscript illustration depicts a castle under siege by troops using cannon and defended by soldiers shielded by temporary wooden palisades (British Library, Royal Ms. 14. E. IV, f. 59v).

Left: Some members of the Don family regained positions of authority: Sir John Don of Kidwelly (d. 1503) was able to commission an altarpiece from the Flemish artist, Hans Memling (d. 1494). The central panel includes portraits of Sir John and his wife (National Gallery, London).

Much of the great gatehouse at Kidwelly remains as completed in 1422 and includes evidence for the change in plans, which can be identified by a careful inspection of the fabric of the building.

those of the hall and the chapel. Such repairs continued on a small scale, with work on the ditches, 'making new hedges [palisades?] for the safe keeping of the castle', and the 'building of a new wooden tower ... where most needed against the Welsh rebels and other French enemies'.

Although the castle was not taken, the town was destroyed. Nevertheless, it was reported that the town defences had been repaired by the December after the 1403 siege, though this seems unlikely, for the town's south gate had been burnt, and it would have been almost impossible to repair it so quickly. In fact the old town, as opposed to the newer settlement across the river, does not appear to have ever fully recovered from the attacks. In 1444, the old town is described in the town charter as 'now in a manner waste and desolate for the want of Burgesses there dwelling', and in the 1530s John Leland wrote that the old, or walled, part of the town 'is nere all desolatid'.

Once the threat from Owain Glyn Dŵr had subsided, building work resumed apace on the gatehouse. Between 1408 and 1421, Duchy of Lancaster records detail expenditure on the building for almost every year, amounting to a total of £500 — equivalent to roughly £200,000 today. However, a study of the surviving documents and the building itself shows that construction must have resumed according to a different plan. Over £14 was paid for 'the digging of stone for the new work of the Tower over the gates', which may refer to the new stair turret that was added to the north-west corner of the gatehouse. Moreover, the plan may have changed more than once. Two of the later accounts (for 1415–16 and 1419–20) mention a fire in the gatehouse, which must have taken place between 1408 and 1415. It seems that at least the roof was destroyed, necessitating 'the repair and mending of the hall and chamber of the great tower over the castle gates of Kidwelly previously burnt'. By 1422, the roof of the gatehouse was covered with lead.

A careful examination of the gatehouse reveals that much more than just the north-west tower was built, though whether the alterations were made before the fire, or were put in place as a result of it, is not clear. Improvements were made to the facilities (additional fireplaces, a new kitchen, and finer windows) and to the means of access to and within the gate. To the front of the gatehouse, most of the main windows from the ground floor upwards were widened to bring in more light. To the rear, the entire wall of the second floor was totally rebuilt, and, on the east side of the first floor, a new kitchen was added, with a large fireplace and oven. Construction of vaulted roofs in 1415–16 — possibly in the new kitchen and the upper floors of the gatehouse — may have been in response to the fire mentioned earlier.

Internally, access arrangements were reorganized, perhaps indicating changes in the control of movement between rooms: the staircase that led from the west guard chamber to the first floor was blocked and a stair turret was built in the north-west corner to link all the floors. The latter may have replaced an earlier arrangement that allowed access to the second floor and battlements. Externally, a grand entrance to the gatehouse was built against the north-east corner of the inner wall, possibly replacing a timber staircase.

The new works to what was known in 1476 as 'the gatehows called the constablery' were refurbishments on a grand scale. In spite of the recent siege, the second phase of the gatehouse (1408–22) reflects a new emphasis on comfort for the seat of Duchy administration. As well as providing improved accommodation suitable for the constable of the king's castle, the refurbished gatehouse, with its impressive arched machicolations high above the entrance, left no doubt that Kidwelly was part and parcel of the machinery of royal authority in the area.

Yet the castle was not entirely without threat at this time. With Henry V away fighting in France, the Duchy's castles were ordered to be specially garrisoned and an additional twelve archers manned Kidwelly from July to December 1415, the year of the Agincourt campaign. The accounts for 1415–16 also record a variety of arms and armour at the castle, including bascinets (a form of helmet), breast plates and chain mail gauntlets, five crossbows, eight bows, twenty-five sheaves of arrows, and three guns — much of which had been sent from London at the time of the recent troubles.

The chapel, too, appears to have been well equipped with a pair of vestments, a chalice, two missals, two cruets (for wine and water) and three bells. There were also 200 shingles left out of a consignment of 6,000, the rest having been used to repair the roofs of towers and other buildings.

As a result of the construction of the new great gate, two stretches of the outer curtain had to be rebuilt, linking the gate to tower 1 on the west side, and on the east to the south-east tower of the inner ward. Either the thirteenth-century curtain could not be keyed into the new gate satisfactorily, or it was felt that the earlier walling did not meet the standards of the day. Stubs of the original curtain to the west of the gatehouse can still be seen up against both tower 1 and the gate.

Repair and Maintenance: The Later Middle Ages and Beyond

As with any building today, routine care and maintenance were needed to prevent the deterioration of the castle, as well as its contents, including such items as arms and armour. Fifteenth-century accounts recording payments for general housekeeping duties in the castle — in the expectation of a visit from the auditors of the Duchy of Lancaster — suggest that the main function

A fifteenth-century silver signet ring from Kidwelly (National Museum of Wales).

Shipping facilities were important to the burgesses of Kidwelly for the export of wool and the import of luxuries not easily available in south Wales; equally important was a quay where building supplies could be unloaded and brought to the castle. This late fifteenth-century manuscript illustration shows a cargo ship unloading at a port (Bodleian Library, Ms. Douce 208, f. 120v).

*J. M. W. Turner (1775–1851)
visited Kidwelly in 1795, when
he sketched the castle twice.
The castle evidently made some
impression on him for it was
not until 1835 that he painted
this watercolour — widely
acknowledged as one of Turner's
finest paintings (Harris Museum
and Art Gallery, Preston).*

of the castle remained administrative. These accounts also reveal a continuing round of minor routine works, and not just to the masonry itself. In the mid-1450s the cleansing and clearing of thorns and furze around the ditch took one man 17 days, at 5*d.* a day.

In 1442–43, the accounts list a great range of repairs, costing almost £26. Wooden laths, boards and shingles from the forest of 'Kevengorath' (Cefn Gorach), from where most of the castle's timber came, were shipped up river to the quay at Kidwelly, and there unloaded and carried up to the castle. It was at this time, too, that the buttresses were added to the west wall of the hall and solar range. A reference to the 'making of a stone wall next to the Constabulary' in 1453–54 may refer to the barbican wall that projects south from the eastern tower of the great gate.

Most of this work would have been carried out by local tradesmen with specialist craftsmen occasionally brought in to sort out specific problems, as happened when John Jeffrey of Coventry was paid to repair a number of defects in the leadwork over the 'New Work', presumably the great gatehouse.

In the later fifteenth century, further buildings were added to the outer ward, suggesting that the medieval accommodation was no longer adequate for either residential or administrative purposes. These buildings may be associated with the works detailed in the accounts for 1478–79 to 1480–81. Large quantities of roofing nails ('lathnails') and shingles were bought from Carmarthen and Bristol, and 20,000 stone slates for roofing were shipped from Ilfracombe, Devon, in the heart of the West Country — a major source of roofing slate for prestige buildings in southern Britain during the Middle Ages. These purchases imply substantial roofing works, which may relate to the new buildings as opposed to existing structures.

The purpose for which some of these later buildings were built is not always clear; however, there is a small lodging against the outer curtain to the north of tower 1, and beyond, close to the north gate, there is a bakehouse with ovens.

There are two other large buildings in the outer ward, which may date from this time. Just to the west of the inner ward, there is a 'hall', and close to the north gate, on the opposite side of the ward from the bakehouse, there is a rectangular building. Again, it is difficult to be certain what these buildings were used for; perhaps the 'hall' is the courthouse mentioned in 1402–03 (p. 17), or even the 'great stable', which is often mentioned amongst the repairs. One stable at least stood close to the north gate: 'the stable next to the little gate' is mentioned in 1520–21 and this two-storey structure could have provided stabling on the ground floor with storage and servant accommodation above.

Tudor accounts of the Duchy of Lancaster also reveal a succession of repairs and minor new works undertaken at the castle. Nevertheless, by 1609, although the king's judicial court still sat in the castle when necessary, Kidwelly had become 'greatly decayed and ruynated'. The Vaughan family of Golden Grove near Llandeilo, Carmarthenshire, acquired the castle in 1630, and Kidwelly seems to have taken no part in the Civil War of the 1640s.

John Vaughan carried out some minor repairs between 1793 and 1802–03, perhaps in response to the increasing numbers of tourists who had begun to visit south Wales. The wars with France, which had convulsed so much of Europe from 1793 onwards, had put an abrupt end to both the aristocratic and aesthetic grand tour in countries such as France and Italy. In response, it was to areas such as the Wye Valley, the Lake District and Wales that tourists and artists alike turned in search of the 'Picturesque' and the 'Sublime'. Many published accounts of these tours of Wales exist. J. T. Barber, writing in 1803, thought that the castle was 'a noble object', and Edward Donovan, two years later, wrote that: 'There is an air of solemn majesty in its appearance, that bespeaks a noble origin.' Kidwelly attracted artists too, perhaps the most famous being J. M. W. Turner (1775–1851), who visited and sketched the castle in 1795.

The castle later passed by descent to the earls of Cawdor, who undertook some repair work to the outer curtain around the middle of the nineteenth century. It was also noted at this time that the wall against the chapel tower had fallen recently: presumably this was the mantlet wall. At about the same time that these minor works were being undertaken, the first modern survey of the castle was made, with plans and elevation drawings made by H. Smyth to accompany G. T. Clark's paper on the castle in *Archaeologia Cambrensis* for 1852.

In 1927, the castle passed into State care and, together with the town gate, is now maintained by Cadw, the historic environment service of the Welsh Assembly Government.

The castle on the eve of repair and consolidation in the 1920s.

This watercolour of Kidwelly Castle, by an unknown artist, shows much of the northern half of the castle completely overgrown and in decay.

A Tour of Kidwelly Castle

The tour is designed to allow visitors to explore the castle at will, noting all the main features of interest. We enter as our medieval counterparts would have done, through the great south gatehouse. From here, the route moves through the outer ward to the inner ward, with its four large round towers, hall and kitchen ranges and chapel tower, though it is possible to visit the various parts of the castle in any order using the bird's-eye view (inside front cover) or the ground plan (inside back cover) as a guide.

The Gatehouse

Exterior

The main entrance to the castle in the later Middle Ages was through the impressive south gatehouse, as it is today. The purpose of the gatehouse was not only to act as a formidable obstacle to would-be intruders, but also to proclaim the lord's status and to provide comfortable, self-contained accommodation appropriate for the king's constable, who would have occupied the fine rooms on the first and second floors.

In all, there are some twenty rooms in the gatehouse, as indicated by the numerous window openings, many of which have been widened to allow more light into the chambers as considerations of comfort became more important. Another indication of the increasing emphasis on comfort is the addition of numerous fireplaces and chimneys, when the second phase of building work began after 1408 (pp. 20–21).

Before entering the gatehouse, however, it is well worth looking at the outside of this impressive building. It consists of five levels: basement, ground floor with first and second floors above, and finally the battlements, most of which have long since disappeared. Although round-fronted towers flank the gate-passage

at the front, the building lacks the symmetry of contemporary castle gatehouses: to the right (east), there is a curved projecting wall, and to the left (west) there is a tall rectangular chamber block.

The short stretch of curtain wall to the right of the gatehouse is probably part of the barbican, or outer defence of the gate, and may have been added as late as the 1450s (p. 22). The barbican protected the area where the castle ditch ran into the scarp and could have been connected to the mound in front of the gatehouse, on which a tower is said to have stood. To the left of the gate the curved line of the Norman ringwork bank is clear; so too is one of the thirteenth-century mural towers (tower 1), and the fifteenth-century section of curtain wall.

The narrow slits in the basement and ground-floor chambers were primarily for light, but perhaps served archers, too, with smaller openings lighting the latrines. The ground-floor rooms at the front have one narrow window apiece, which were widened from slits during the second phase of building work, as were the marginally larger windows that lit the chambers above. The one exception is the first-floor window above the entrance, where the original embrasure appears to have been partially blocked, and a new smaller window inserted.

Between the two towers, the arched doorway is set in a rectangular recess into which the drawbridge would have been raised, lifted by chains or ropes running through the small square holes in the top corners of the recess. When lowered, the drawbridge would have been level — unlike the modern sloping bridge. High above the entrance are three arches known as machicolations, similar to those to be seen at Carmarthen Castle, and part of the finishing touches put to the gate in the early fifteenth century. The machicolations allowed soldiers on the roof of the gatehouse to drop missiles, such as rocks, on to an enemy who might be trying to break down the castle gates. The garrison could even

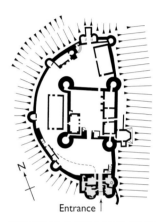

Entrance

Above: The barbican wall abutting the east tower of the gatehouse — 'the Constabulary' — may not have been built until the 1450s.

Opposite: The imposing south face of the great gatehouse, which took more than thirty years to complete. Not only did the gatehouse present a formidable external façade, but it also provided numerous comfortable chambers for the constable of the castle and other retainers of the Duchy of Lancaster.

A reconstruction showing how the machicolations high above the entrance might have been used during an attack on the gatehouse (Illustration by John Banbury, 1986).

Above: The series of holes — especially visible on the east tower of the gatehouse and adjacent curtain — are known as putlog holes and were used to support horizontal scaffolding timbers when the castle was being built.

Right: The early fifteenth-century gatehouse at nearby Carmarthen Castle was built to a very similar design to that at Kidwelly — perhaps reflecting the influence of the same hand at both castles.

pour down water to extinguish fires lit by besiegers trying to burn down the doors.

Although most of the battlements, or crenellations, have been destroyed, it is clear that they were supported on a series of small projecting stones, or corbels, which allowed the masons to build a wider wall-walk behind than would otherwise have been possible. This technique was used in most parts of the castle where crenellations were constructed. Also visible on the outside of the gate, and elsewhere in the castle, is a series of regularly spaced holes. These are putlog holes, and although they are now partially blocked, they originally held the horizontal scaffolding timbers used when the gate was under construction.

Interior

The gatehouse offered a series of obstacles that had to be overcome before the enemy could reach the interior of the castle. On the outside, the would-be intruders were faced with a raised drawbridge, archers firing from the openings in the towers, rocks dropped from the machicolations above and the outer portcullis. This was a heavy wooden grille, perhaps sheathed with iron, which would have been lowered into position down the vertical grooves that are visible just in front of the present gates.

Even if the intruders had managed to enter the gate-passage, further missiles would have rained down from a rectangular slot, or murder hole, in the ceiling of the passage, just behind the gates. There were two more murder holes further along the passage; the one in the centre, however, was blocked, probably after 1408 (pp. 20–21). At the far end of the passage there was another set of doors and a second portcullis. If these obstacles were not enough, the enemy would have been further harassed by the castle's garrison in the rooms on either side of the passage.

Basement

Each tower has a basement, which is accessed directly from the gate-passage. That in the east tower (room 1) is entered from the first door on the right and that in the left (west) tower (room 2) is entered through the middle of three doors. These rooms were probably prison cells, for the inner doors to the basements were secured by drawbars on the outside.

Both basement chambers are lit by one or more slits, and both contain recesses that were latrines. Although archers might have been able to use the arrowslits to cover the ditch around the gate, they would have had to stand on some form of timber platform behind the embrasures. This suggests that the prime purpose of the slits was to provide light and perhaps to act as a deterrent rather than as a serious defensive measure.

Ground Floor

At ground-floor level, the east tower has two chambers, which are directly accessed from the gate-passage. That at the farther end of the passage gave access to the castle's strongroom. In contrast, there are three chambers in the west tower, only two of which are accessible from the gate-passage; the third can be reached via either of the other two rooms. Unlike the basement, all but one of the ground-floor chambers could be locked on the inside, the exception being the strongroom.

The centre door on the right side of the gate-passage leads, via a short corridor, into the chamber (room 4) at the front of the east tower, and is lit by a window with two seats, with two slits covering the area in front of the entrance to the gatehouse. There is a fireplace, which probably dates from the second building phase (1408–22), but no latrine. In the vaulted ceiling above the two slits there is evidence of timber shuttering, where wooden planking has been secured against the original fresh plaster whilst it dried. The planks have left a series of long rectangular impressions in the plaster. This is a useful reminder that most of the rooms would have had a coating of plaster, and it is something that should be looked for elsewhere in the castle.

The third door on the right leads, via an inner door which is lockable on the outside or passage side, into a room (5) that at first glance looks as if it houses the castle's well. On looking down into the 'well' it is apparent that it is no such thing, but a large and bare pit (room 3), once thought to be the castle's main prison. This pit, however, was the strongroom for valuables, the room above being the office for the receiver, or cofferer, and his staff, who looked after the lord's financial matters. The office was provided with a latrine and the slit window is contrived to throw a shaft of light on to a desk or lectern in the middle of the room. Both office and strongroom were essential requirements for any castle that was the administrative centre of a lordship. Nevertheless, although mentioned in medieval records, the whereabouts of the well is not known.

Ground Floor

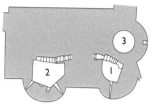

Basement

The circular opening in the floor of the office (room 5) on the ground floor of the gatehouse was the only means of access to the strongroom (room 3) below, built to contain money and valuables. The office, too, could be locked from the outside.

This reconstruction of the great gatehouse is cutaway to show the layout of the rooms, and how the drawbridge and portcullis might have been operated. Above the gate-passage at the back of the gatehouse is the hall with the solar, or private chamber, above (Illustration by Chris Jones-Jenkins, 1986).

One of the slit windows in the receiver's office was subsequently blocked in the early fifteenth century by the addition of the stone staircase leading from the outer ward to the first floor of the gatehouse. Of the various small holes and sockets in the walls of the room, some of which are probably putlog holes, a series in the top of one wall suggests that the ceiling may originally have been timbered. Although the sockets are not substantial enough to have held large beams for a main floor above, they may represent the floor joists of a small loft added later.

The first door on the left of the gate-passage leads into the western ground-floor chamber (room 6) — possibly a porter's lodge — via a short passage and a second or inner door. Two slits cover the front of the gate, above which there is further evidence for timber shuttering, and a passage in the thickness of the wall leads to a latrine lit by a small slit. The positioning of the latrine in the front wall is rather surprising as its presence weakens the front of the tower.

The main window is provided with a seat on each side of the embrasure and holes in the side of the window itself show that originally it held a metal grille or glazing bars for glass. There is also a fireplace, which may be a later addition. Although this was the porter's lodge or guardroom, the facilities in this chamber bespeak some degree of comfort. Off the main room are the remains of the original staircase to the first floor which was blocked in the early fifteenth century and probably replaced by the stair turret in the north-west corner of the building (p. 21). The rectangular recesses at the back of the room were cupboards.

The impression of timber shuttering, where wooden planks have been secured against wet plaster whilst it dries, can be seen above the windows in both ground-floor chambers in the gatehouse (rooms 4 and 6).

The ground-floor chamber (room 6) in the western gatehouse tower may have served as a porter's lodge. It was comfortably equipped with a latrine, fireplace and window with seats.

From the adjacent rectangular chamber (room 8), which is lit by two slits, the stair turret leads to the floor above. Over the door to the stair turret there is evidence for the blocking of an original opening caused by the insertion of the new stairs. In the same room, a door led into another ground-floor chamber (room 7), which can also be entered by the third door on the left in the gate-passage. This room contains a fireplace and a blocked door set into what had been a window.

Leaving the gate-passage, on the right is a rectangular chamber (room 9), backing on to the rear of the receiver's office. Its purpose is uncertain, but with a window and fireplace it may have been an inner porter's lodge.

Once inside the outer ward, the advantages of the concentric castle plan are immediately obvious. To the left, the curving line of the outer curtain wall is overlooked by the towers of the inner ward, so that anyone attacking the castle from the west would be covered by a double line of defences.

Turning to look at the back of the gatehouse, it is clear that the tall rectangular stair turret is an addition to the bulk of the rear wall, butting against it. The windows — some of which retain their finely dressed mouldings — belong to the second building phase, as does much of the walling at second-floor level. On the first floor, the large windows with cusped heads light the hall — a spacious chamber that was used by the constable of the castle, perhaps even as the courthouse, which is mentioned on numerous occasions in the Duchy of Lancaster records, but so far has not been identified. On the floor above, the windows light the private apartments such as the solar, or private sitting room, and the bedchamber, something to which the king's constable was entitled as an important official of the Duchy of Lancaster.

Upper Floors

A flight of steps now leads from the outer ward to the first floor of the gatehouse. This staircase may have replaced an earlier timber arrangement or else it marks the break in building between 1403 and 1408 identified elsewhere in the gatehouse. The first- and second-floor chambers appear to have been considerably altered during the second

Once inside the outer ward, the advantages of concentric planning are clear: the tall towers of the inner ward overlook the curving line of the outer curtain wall towards the landward approach to the castle beyond.

The rear elevation of the great gatehouse. The north-west tower, to the right, and much of the upper floor was built during the second phase of construction between 1408 and 1422. The large windows on the first floor, which were also remodelled in the second building phase, lit the hall.

phase of building work (1408–22). In particular, windows and fireplaces have been inserted and access between rooms and floors has been altered — perhaps in response to different patterns of social circulation within the gatehouse — which make it difficult to understand both the original and modified arrangements.

The staircase leads into what would have been a passage, or antechamber, screening the entrance and the kitchen from the hall (room 15). The room on the left is the kitchen (room 10), which would have enabled the constable and other household officers to be totally self-sufficient in the gatehouse, providing that a supply of water could be maintained. The kitchen, which was remodelled sometime after 1408, is vaulted and roofed in stone, presumably to minimize the risk of fire. It contains a large fireplace with most of its hood missing, and an oven with a further flue above, which replaced an earlier fireplace. One window lights the room, and below it is the drain

for the disposal of kitchen waste. There is also a cupboard.

From the kitchen, a very narrow doorway leads to the wide south-east curtain wall, and thence to the south-east tower of the inner ward. This door was not as secure as its equivalent on the other side of the gatehouse, which opens on to the west curtain wall and was secured by a pair of drawbars, but perhaps the latter was considered the more vulnerable of the two.

The thickness of the south-east curtain wall permits a wide wall-walk, originally protected by battlements on either side, known as a parapet on the outer side and a parados on the inner face. At the far end, the wall-walk breaks into the south-east tower of the inner ward via what may have been a latrine originally. This link aided communication between the inner ward and the gatehouse, especially if an enemy had succeeded in occupying the outer ward. It is from this wall-walk that one is able to obtain the best view of the sacristy attached to the chapel tower (p. 44).

The oven and fireplace in the first-floor kitchen of the gatehouse (room 10).

The hall (room 15) on the first floor of the gatehouse, with the solar (room 21) above. The letters refer to features described in the text.

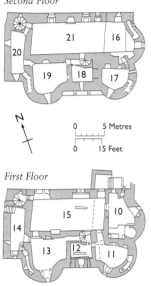

Second Floor

N

0   5 Metres

0   15 Feet

First Floor

Returning to the main first-floor room of the gatehouse (room 15), this would have been divided into two parts: an antechamber, or passage, and a hall at the west end of the room, perhaps separated by a timber screen. In the area occupied by the hall, the socket for the inner portcullis is located in the floor of the eastern window embrasure (A), and there is a murder hole in the floor. Beyond, the hall was equipped with a fireplace and another larger window and it was probably at this end of the room that the constable would have sat at the high table. The ceiling of the hall range was of timber, with the main beams originally set in large sockets and supported by stone corbels halfway up the wall (B). Above the line of this ceiling lay the private apartment, the

solar (room 21), which had a central fireplace in the outside wall (C), with a lamp bracket on each side. A sloping groove cut into the stair turret (D) at the west end of the solar marks the line of the roof — no doubt the one which was finished with lead in 1422.

Two of the other top-floor rooms had timber roofs: the room (19) at the front of the west tower and the small chamber to the east of the solar (16). The latter, equipped with a window, fireplace and small door to a latrine, may have been a bedroom, originally divided from the solar by a timber partition or screen. All of the other second-floor rooms were roofed or vaulted in stone.

Opposite the door at the head of the staircase from the outer ward is the entrance to the first-floor room (11) at the front of the east tower, furnished with window, fireplace, latrine and cupboard. Its ceiling of timber has long since gone, enabling the visitor to see up into the room above (17), which was similarly furnished but roofed in stone; a short passage connected this upper chamber with the presumed bedchamber (16). In the short entrance passage to room 11, there is a blocked door that originally led to room 12, and adjacent to this is a chimney flue, which leads from the fireplace in the floor below to a chimney at roof level.

The next doorway, on the left, enters a passage leading to the central front room (12), which contains the outer murder hole above the gate-passage below. The mechanisms for raising the drawbridge and the outer portcullis would have been located here and/or in the room above (18) (see reconstruction, p. 28).

Outside the portcullis chamber, steps lead to a staircase that may have been part of the original build, and to a passage that connects with the rooms in the west tower. The staircase continued up to the solar (21) (entered through a fine ogee-headed doorway) and adjacent chambers. The first-floor room (13) in the west tower, like those above and below it, is larger than the equivalent in the east tower. The chamber has a window and a fireplace, but no latrine; for this, one had to go into the adjacent rectangular chamber (room 14), where a mural passage houses a latrine as in the floor below. The door at the far end of this room leads to the outer curtain wall, and just outside, on the wall-walk, the stubs of some walling set in the stair turret may mark the height of the original inner battlements. Above room 14, corbels indicate where the builders have squeezed in two small plastered rooms (20), the lower entered through a door off the stair turret, and the upper from the main front room (19) on the second floor.

From room 13, the hall (15) is entered through a door that is a later addition, probably part of the second phase of the fifteenth-century alterations, when the stone staircase from the outer ward was added. It replaced an earlier door, the blocking for which is visible to the left and above the existing door, framed in white Sutton Stone. The remaining door from the hall enters the stair turret, which continued up to the rooms above and opened out on to the battlements, an area now inaccessible to visitors.

The Outer Ward

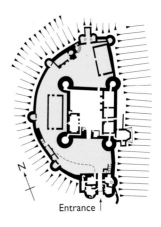

The outer ward of the castle served two purposes: in the thirteenth century it would have acted primarily as a killing zone should the outer walls have been breached; by the fifteenth century it would also have housed more ancillary buildings, such as stables. The enemy who gained entry into this area would have been at the mercy of the garrison in the inner ward, as well as those defenders still resisting from along the outer circuit.

Essentially, the outer ward is a large D-shaped enclosure, which surrounds a compact, square inner ward. To the west, it is protected by a curving curtain wall, with three mural towers, between gatehouses to the north and south. To the east, above the steep slope to the river, a curtain wall links the two gatehouses by way of the inner ward and a fourth mural tower at the north-east corner.

Part of the curving D-shaped outer curtain wall and one of the mural towers (3) that protected the outer ward.

This large rectangular building in the outer ward, opposite the middle mural tower (2), has been identified as a courthouse, though it could have been the 'great stable', the location of which is also unknown.

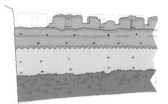

Late twelfth/
early thirteenth century

Late thirteenth century

Early fourteenth century

Three phases of construction are preserved in the outer curtain wall, between towers 2 and 3. The lowest third dates from the end of the twelfth or the beginning of the thirteenth century; the middle section was raised almost a hundred years later by the Chaworth brothers, and the corbelled parapet was probably built in the early fourteenth century.

The mural towers along the curtain wall are all of a similar design, with three floors equipped with arrowslits covering the ditch and flanking each other as well as the curtain walls to either side of them. They were battlemented at the top, with a wall-walk that originally ran continuously along the outer curtain wall. At least one chamber in each tower has a fireplace, so clearly they were intended to be occupied, especially after their backs were constructed in stone to replace timber-framed walls (pp. 11, 14).

The internal arrangements can best be seen in the southern tower (tower 1), that nearest the great gatehouse. Here, a first-floor fireplace at the front of the tower is adjacent to a passage leading to a latrine, which projected out from the tower wall, supported on corbels. Between this latrine and the back wall of the tower is a blocked doorway that led into a passage within the curtain wall, and which was provided with two arrowslits, visible from outside the castle. The narrowness of the passage meant that only crossbows could have been used by archers.

Between tower 1 and the steps that lead to the wall-walk, there is a late medieval lodging with a fireplace and two chambers. There may have been another staircase on the south side of tower 3, where a stub of masonry protrudes from high up on the face of the curtain.

Between the middle tower (2), the front of which has long since collapsed, and the inner ward is a rectangular building, which has tentatively been identified as a courthouse. Alternatively, it could have been the 'great stable', the location of which is otherwise unknown. Only the gable ends, each with doors set in them, survive to any extent. Squeezed in between this building and the inner curtain wall are the foundations of a latrine block.

The curtain wall between towers 2 and 3 contains evidence for three phases in the castle's development. The lowest third is the earliest masonry that survives at Kidwelly, dating to around the end of the twelfth or the beginning of the thirteenth century (p. 9);

between this masonry and the early fourteenth-century corbelled parapet is the curtain built by the Chaworths in the later thirteenth century.

Between tower 3 and the north gatehouse is a late medieval bakehouse, containing the remains of two large ovens, one of which now lacks its domed roof. The distinct gap between the end wall of the bakehouse and the outer curtain demonstrates that this building was a later addition.

Little remains of the small north gatehouse, except for one of its two D-shaped towers, which still rises to first-floor level. Originally, these towers may have been timber-backed like the adjacent mural towers. A few slits, however, survive including one on the outer face of the east tower, which is not visible internally. Three drainage channels cut into the gate-passage also survive. The upper levels of the gatehouse were reached by steps and a passage in the western curtain. To the east, a mural passage gave access to the tower at the north-east corner of the castle.

Parallel walls project from the front of the gate, flanking the turning bridge that crossed the ditch. A masonry pier — onto which the drawbridge would have been lowered — stands on the other side of the ditch. From the outside, the original battlements of the short stretch of the curtain wall to the east are clear, although now blocked. The raising of the curtain wall here is cruder than elsewhere in the castle.

Beyond the gate lie the earthworks of the north ward or bailey. The bank and ditch, which cut off the extreme end of the enclosure, were dug soon after the siege during the Glyn Dŵr revolt (p. 18). Although this area may have been part of the castle's defences in the twelfth century, it later served a more domestic purpose, for it contained gardens and a dovecote. At some date, certainly in the post-medieval period, two rabbit warrens were established in this area; warrens, along with dovecotes, provided an important supply of fresh meat.

At the north-east corner of the outer curtain, a wall has been built across the back of what little remains of a small mural tower (tower 4), thus obscuring it from view. The curtain wall continues from tower 4 to the north-east tower of the inner ward and, although it appears to be largely of thirteenth-century date, there have been later alterations. Against the curtain wall is a further

late medieval rectangular building. There are windows, with seats, in each of the gable ends at first-floor level, which was presumably reached by a timber staircase, but few other features remain to indicate the purpose of the building, though documents of 1520–21 do refer to the 'stable next to the little gate'. The ground floor could have served as a stable, with storage and accommodation above.

Above: Part of the late medieval bakehouse built against the outer curtain wall, adjacent to the north gatehouse.

Left: Little remains of the small north gatehouse, which was probably built by the Chaworths in the later thirteenth century and opened into the north bailey.

Another late medieval building — perhaps the 'stable next to the little gate' — was built against the outer curtain in the north-east corner of the outer ward.

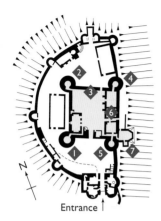

Entrance ↑

The inner ward consists of a small square courtyard surrounded by curtain walls with a large round tower at each corner — each built to a different design — and entered via two quite simple gates. Within the enclosure lay domestic buildings and a chapel.

The Inner Ward

The inner ward is accessible through two simple gateways, one to the north and one to the south. It consists of a square courtyard surrounded by a curtain wall with one large round tower at each corner — each different in design and each equipped to provide a variety of accommodation. Within the courtyard itself lay the lord's domestic accommodation, chapel and kitchen.

The round towers have thick, slightly splayed bases, designed to act both as supports and, possibly, as a deterrent to undermining in time of siege. There are several tiers of arrowslits enabling archers in the towers to cover the open ground within the outer ward. These slits have been constructed in a variety of ways: some framed in dressed stone or ashlar, some partially in dressed stone, and others dressed not at all. The designs vary as well; some have horizontal slits which gave archers a greater viewing

area. The blocked rectangular openings near the tops of the towers of the inner ward represent the original late thirteenth-century battlements; and both the northern towers were also equipped with hourds at this time. When the towers were raised, the stairs were carried up to the roofs and capped with turrets. The small holes running below the present battlements drained the roofs.

The north and south gates were not very sophisticated. Originally, each had one door and a portcullis operated from above, but, set as they were between two massive towers, they did not require greater sophistication. The north gate was particularly well protected by numerous arrowslits in the north-west tower. A similar arrangement can be seen at Conwy Castle, built by Edward I in the 1280s. The rear part of the south gate was added slightly later to provide support for the open staircase, which leads up to the wall-walk that runs around the ward. Note that only the inner battlements (parados) of the curtain wall are set on corbels.

The South-West Tower

This tower, known as the Julian Tower in the early fifteenth century, is unique in that the upper floors are stone vaulted. Today, the chambers in this tower are reached from a medieval staircase accessible from the wall-walk, via the steps alongside the south gate. Originally, there was access to the ground floor of the south-west tower from behind the kitchen range. This chamber, now inaccessible to visitors, was lit by three arrowslits, and lay over a basement (perhaps used as a prison). This was lit by two small slits high up in the wall with embrasures sloping down to allow as much light into the basement as possible. In the Middle Ages, the only way to have reached the basement was through a trap-door from the floor above, and a similar arrangement existed in the north-west tower.

The first floor of the tower has two arrowslits and a fireplace; the room above has only one slit and an arched recess leading to a latrine, the base of whose chute is visible on the outside of the tower. Originally, the chute would have opened into a pit at the base of the wall, which some unfortunate would have had to clean out periodically. The uppermost or third floor has a fireplace and two arrowslits. The large corbels or stones projecting from the wall, which are such a prominent feature, would have supported the timbers of the original roof of the tower before it was raised in the late thirteenth or early fourteenth century.

The stairs continue to the battlements and the dome-shaped roof. Some steps originally ran up the turret to its own set of battlements, thus providing an excellent observation post for a sentry. The equivalent turret on the north-west tower is an even better example. From the top of the tower, the layout of the early medieval town can be traced in the modern streets to the south of the castle, including the south gate and the town wall and ditch, which runs westwards from the castle's ditch.

From the roof of the south-west tower, it can best be appreciated why the towers of the inner ward had to be raised after the Lancastrian heightening of the outer curtain. Archers on the top of the two western towers, in particular, were able to cover the castle ditch, which would not have been possible from the room below — the approximate level of the original battlements built by the Chaworths.

The North-West Tower  and Curtain Wall

The flooring of the remaining three towers no longer exists; nevertheless it is still possible to identify differences in the provision and quality of the accommodation in each.

The north-west tower (called Maugrey Meredith's Tower in the fifteenth century) is a distinctive 'kidney shape' in plan, formed by two spiral staircases either side of a recess in the back wall. From the wall-walk, the internal arrangements of each floor level can be seen, marked by projecting stone corbels. Here, too, the basement may have been a prison. Above, the first-floor entrance to the tower was reached from the inner ward, and it seems to have been enclosed within a small building, the foundations of which survive against the west and north curtains. Of all the battlements on the towers of the inner ward, those on the north-west tower are the best preserved.

In the north section of the wall-walk, the slot for the portcullis of the north gate can be seen. The battlements of the curtain wall in this area show the original defensive arrangement which enabled archers to fire through gaps

The south-west tower of the inner ward. The blocked late thirteenth-century battlements are clearly visible, fossilized in the masonry when the tower was later raised with a corbelled parapet.

The upper floor of the south-west tower — the only tower to be vaulted in stone. The room contains a fireplace and two arrowslits.

in the crenellations, as well as through slits in the merlons. There is hardly room to draw a longbow comfortably here, and it may be that crossbowmen would have manned these walls in time of need.

The North-East Tower

The north-east tower was called the Lord's Tower in 1402, an appropriate name for a structure that adjoined the lord's solar at the north end of the hall range. This is the one tower whose raised battlements are not supported on a series of corbels; and there are sockets for a timber hourd or projecting gallery. On the north-east side of the tower is a good example of a spout that drained rainwater from the battlements.

The chamber above the basement has a short passage leading to the river side of the tower, seemingly to gain access to the area enclosed by the mantlet wall or even a covered passage to the chapel. A timber staircase or ladder would have led down from the outer door of the passage. Originally, however, in the late thirteenth century the passage may have led to a corridor built within the curtain wall, similar to that leading from tower 1 in the outer ward.

The basement of the north-east tower is reached by its own door, probably to access storage, and there are fireplaces on the second and third floors. The tower was also provided with a latrine, the chute of which opened down the natural slope outside the walls.

A fifteenth-century reference mentions a chapel in this tower, perhaps a private place of worship for the use of the lord and his family.

The South-East Tower and Hall Range

Both of the eastern towers of the inner ward — those furthest from the more vulnerable western curtain — were well positioned at either end of the hall range to provide accommodation for the owners of the castle.

The south-east tower is especially well furnished with a fireplace on each of the upper floors, unlike its counterparts in the inner ward. Before the hall and solar range were built, this tower probably served as accommodation for the lord of the castle. Once the hall was in place, this tower would have been at the lower — or less prestigious — end of the range and service rooms probably occupied the lowest levels with guest chambers above.

The basement was reached by a door under the hall and lit originally by two slits. The room above is entered by the right-hand of three doors, the thresholds of which are virtually at the same level. An opening in the left wall of the passage leading from the door on the right would have connected with the stairs to the upper levels of the tower, the main access to which was the middle door. This connecting

The north-east tower adjoined the solar end of the hall block, the roofline of which can be traced on the inner face of the tower.

A section of the curtain wall between the north-west and north-east towers. Although archers could fire through gaps in the crenellations as well as slits in the merlons, the cramped conditions probably favoured the use of crossbows rather than longbows.

Opposite: The north-west tower is distinguished by its unusual 'kidney shape', created by two spiral staircases, one either side of a recess in the back wall. The battlements are especially well preserved on this tower.

The Town and Town Defences

The best-preserved section of the town wall runs from the edge of the castle ditch, where it appears to terminate, opposite the fallen mural tower (2).

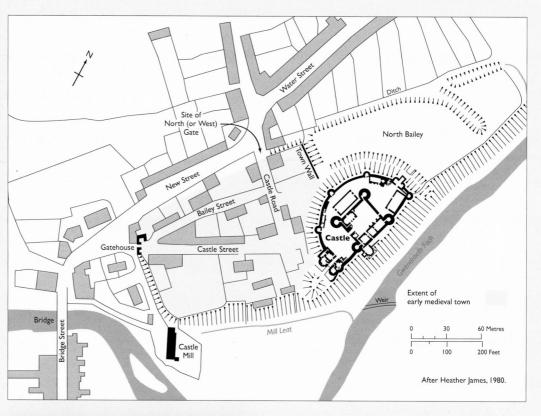

After Heather James, 1980.

The town's south gate is still a prominent feature and dates from about 1300.

The small medieval borough of Kidwelly seems to have grown up as a garrison town more or less coeval with the castle. Like the castle, its earliest defences were built of earth and timber, but these were replaced in stone after the first murage grant of 1280. The town was granted its first charter in 1308 and it was confirmed in 1357. With the right to hold two markets a week and one annual fair, Kidwelly's commercial success was assured.

As a result, the town soon outgrew the confined area of the southern bailey and instead developed around the Benedictine priory on the opposite side of the river. By 1401, Duchy of Lancaster officials described the walled town as 'ruinous, waste, and desolate'. Despite attempts to revive the old town — with ordinances ordering the repair of houses, burgesses (English only) to be present, and markets to be held within its walls — the tide of change could not be reversed, and after the town was destroyed in 1403 (p. 20), it seems never to have fully recovered.

The line of the original defences can, however, still be traced in roads and property boundaries; indeed parts of the town wall and ditch, and the south gate still survive. The best-preserved section of wall runs from the edge of the castle ditch, opposite mural tower 2, and the town ditch in front of it is still a prominent feature.

John Leland, in his brief description of Kidwelly in the 1530s, mentions that the town had three gates. Two have been identified: the south gate at the end of Castle Street, which survives to a substantial height and the north (or west) gate, which seems to have been located at the end of Castle Road, though no trace of it survives. The archway in the lane leading to the north bailey is of a much later date, perhaps designed to provide access to the north bailey and its rabbit warrens. The site of the third gate is less clear, though it seems likely that a gate — perhaps just a postern — lay close to the mound opposite the castle's main entrance. This could be the gate near the 'big gate' of the castle for which a lock was bought in 1479.

The south gate dates from around 1300; it is rectangular in plan with towers on either side of the gateway, each having chamfered sides and spur buttresses. Grooves for a portcullis and sockets for a drawbar indicate how the gate was made secure.

The gatehouse originally consisted of a ground floor with two upper storeys, but was seriously damaged in 1403 (p. 20); by the 1530s John Leland describes the gate as 'the ruins of a fair town haul, and under a prison'.

Later buildings obscure much of the western part of the south gate, and the loss of the rear wall makes interpretation of the interior difficult. Although the ground-floor chambers were equipped with arrowslits, there are no traces of medieval fireplaces or latrines, perhaps suggesting that these rooms were not designed for permanent residence. There were three chambers at first-floor level and the town hall mentioned by Leland may have occupied the second floor. By this time the portcullis slot had been partially blocked — perhaps during later fifteenth-century refurbishment — indicating that the gate had a less obvious defensive role.

door was later blocked so that the private chambers could be kept totally separate from a room now used by domestic staff, perhaps as the pantry, where bread and tableware for the hall would have been stored and prepared for service. By this time, the basement would probably have served as the buttery and/or a cellar for wine or ale. The door to the left leads into the chapel tower. The purpose of the two recesses to the right of the doors is not known for certain, but the smaller of the two would probably have contained a basin for washing hands before entering the hall.

The south-east tower was originally designed to accommodate the Chaworth family within the security of the inner ward of their private fortress. However, when the castle became the seat of local administration for the Duchy of Lancaster, the tower was modified to fulfil a new role — as demonstrated by the changes both to the access arrangements and to its name. The accounts for repairs in 1442–43 refer to it as the Exchequer Tower, so called presumably because it held the regional financial and other records of the Duchy of Lancaster. The close proximity of the Duchy's auditor — who seems to have occupied a room beneath the chapel, sometimes called the Auditor's Chamber, during his frequent visits — perhaps confirms this.

Between the two eastern towers is a large late thirteenth- or early fourteenth-century range, which contained the hall and the solar, or private sitting room (north end), at first-floor level. The outer wall

An artist's impression of how the hall range may have looked, after the buttresses were added to the northern end some time in the middle of the fifteenth century (Illustration by Chris Jones-Jenkins, 1986).

The hall range looking towards the solar end and the north-east tower. Both the hall and solar would have been located at first-floor level.

Numerous doorways lead into the much-altered south-east tower from the hall range: each may have allowed discrete access by different members of the ducal household for domestic and residential use. The pillar in the foreground probably supported a central hearth in the hall above.

of the range is built on the slightly earlier curtain wall raised by the Chaworths, the remains of which are clear at basement level. The roof line of the hall against the south-east tower is very clear; so too is that of the solar on the face of the north-east tower.

Inside the solar little remains except for a fireplace and lancet window on the east, or river, side, and the evidence for another window. The height of the roof meant that the chimney, too, would have been very tall, perhaps akin to the fourteenth-century chimney at Grosmont in Monmouthshire, which was part of the refurbishment of that castle by the earls of Lancaster. A rough recess in the inner, or west, wall of the solar marks the site of the door that led into the hall, though it now lacks the dressed stones of the door jamb.

The hall itself was a large, steep-roofed building, and would have been extremely impressive when completed; in size it compares favourably with near-contemporary halls, such as that at Gilbert de Clare's Caerphilly. The hall itself would have had a central fireplace (probably supported on a circular pillar, the remains of which survive in the basement) with a stone wall at the north end, dividing it from the solar.

The area below the hall and solar was used as a wine and ale cellar, and was lit by small windows facing the inner ward. The main door into the basement was under the solar. Under the hall, a passage led from the courtyard to the east side of the castle, with doors at each end, the inner one being marked by two carved door jamb stops at floor level. Doors off this passage also led into the storerooms.

Most of the internal features of the basement probably date to a later period, and include a stone tank; this was a malt kiln. The buttresses supporting the courtyard wall of the hall range seem to be those recorded in accounts for 1442–43. At the south end of the building, between the hall and the south gate, are the curving foundations of the stairs that would have led to the first-floor hall. Between these foundations and the curtain wall is the site of a small room — referred to as 'the little kitchen at the door of the king's hall' in 1442–43. However, with the large contemporary kitchen across the courtyard, this room may have been an area for the final preparation of dishes before they were taken into the hall. Alternatively, it could have been used as a privy — private — kitchen for the preparation of the lord's meals. To the left of the fireplace in this room is the remaining jamb of the doorway that led into the passage that would have taken servants into the hall.

Spur buttresses became a distinctive feature of castles in Wales and the Marches about 1300. Goodrich Castle, Herefordshire (far left) and the north dam at Caerphilly Castle, Glamorgan (left) are two particularly good examples (Goodrich — English Heritage).

Below: Kidwelly's chapel tower projects beyond the line of the curtain wall, supported on two massive spur buttresses, on the scarp slope running down to the river.

The Chapel Tower

The chapel is one of the finest features of the castle, dating from the extensive refurbishment that took place at the end of the thirteenth century; it must therefore have replaced an earlier site of worship of which nothing now remains. The tower projects boldly from the south-east wall of the hall range, down the scarp towards the river Gwendraeth. The chapel thus served as a flanking tower to cover the east curtain wall, but was probably built down the scarp simply because there was no room to build such an elaborate structure anywhere else.

The two massive spur buttresses against the east wall of the tower support and strengthen the building, and can best be appreciated from outside the castle. These spur buttresses can also be seen at other castles of about 1300 in Wales and the Marches, such as Carreg Cennen (Carmarthenshire), Goodrich (Herefordshire) and Caerphilly.

The north wall of the chapel was built, for the most part, against the existing thirteenth-century masonry, the two walls merging as one at the top. Part of the mantlet wall projects from the tower's north wall, and on the outside where the two meet there is a blocked ashlar-faced arrowslit, perhaps indicating a change of plan as the tower was under construction.

The tower consists of a basement and ground floor with the chapel itself on the upper floor. Originally, the basement probably served a military function and the castle chaplain used the floor above.

However, as rebuilt around 1441–42 the basement or 'the bulke' appears to have been designed as a secure room accessible only from what was now the auditor's private chamber on the floor above.

The chapel would have been used by the Lancaster family when in residence, and by senior Duchy officials visiting the castle. And although Mass appears to have been said on behalf of the departed (pp. 13–14), it is clear from the annual accounts that the chapel was not in constant use.

The entrance to the chapel was through a door in the north wall, which may have been accessed via a gallery with a pentice, or lean-to, roof that ran from the north-east tower to the chapel, within the mantlet wall. Inside, the chapel was lit by two tiers of trefoil-headed lancet windows, finely dressed with white Sutton Stone (from near Southerndown in the Vale of Glamorgan) in stark contrast to the other masonry used in the building. Between the clerestory (upper) windows are the corbels which would have supported the roof timbers of the chapel. In the south wall, to the right of the site of the altar, there is a double piscina, a basin in which the sacred vessels were washed after Mass, and a wide sedile, a seat for the use of the priest.

Unusually, there is no surviving evidence for wall painting in the chapel, suggesting that the walls were plain white.

It is not possible to be certain of the original arrangements at ground-floor level, though doors in each of the north and west walls appear to be original features. The modern entrance is via a window that was later widened to create a door. A door in the thickness of the east wall allowed access to the basement.

The small building on the south side of the tower contained the sacristy, which was entered by a door to the right of the sedile, or priest's seat; beyond the door a window has been blocked. Below the sacristy is a small room with access to a latrine contained in the south wall of the tower itself. The sacristy has a fine, stone cruciform roof that is best appreciated from the curtain wall leading from the kitchen of the great gate. This small building housed the vessels used in the Mass, and we know that in the fifteenth century the sacristy held candelabra, cups or chalices, a bell and various vestments stored in a coffer. Altar cloths were also stored here and were cleaned or washed regularly at a cost of 4d. before the arrival of the auditor.

The East Side of the Castle

There are several features of interest on the east side of the castle, visible from the footpath that runs from the left of the monument to Gwenllian (p. 7), beyond the south gatehouse, down the slope and along the river frontage.

At the base of the projecting elliptical section of the gate is the opening of the latrine chute from the strongroom (1). High above, the remains of the corbelled latrine serving the small chamber at the end of the solar on the top floor of the gatehouse can also be made out (2). Between the gatehouse and the south-east tower of the inner ward, there is what looks like a blocked opening with an arch at the bottom of the wall. There was in fact no opening here; this feature is known as a relieving arch, designed to support the masonry above an area of potential weakness, so presumably the foundations were considered to be unstable at this point (3).

Beyond the latrine chute in the south-east tower (4), and the small building containing the sacristy (5), is the front of the chapel tower (6) with its massive spur buttresses and latrine chute (7). At the top of the spur on the right there is a small cross-slit which lights the staircase; nearby the mantlet wall almost obscures a slit flanking the north-east side of the castle (p. 43).

The tallest part of the hall range is the base of the chimney of the solar (8), and on the side of it are traces of the original line of the sloping roof. Next to the solar is the doorway (9), which may have led to a timber passage to the chapel (pp. 39, 44). Further along, on the north side of the north-east tower of the inner ward, is the base of a latrine chute, adjacent to one of the tower's arrowslits covering the curtain wall to the north. At the extreme end of the castle are the remains of the small mural tower (10) not visible from the inner ward because of the wall built across it at a later date (p. 35). Downslope from this are the remains of the wing-wall that protected the end of the ditch.

A small cross-slit lights the staircase in the chapel tower.

The remains of the small mural tower at the north-east corner of the outer ward.

Left: The impressive east face of Kidwelly Castle, high above the river Gwendraeth.

The Remaining Buildings in the Inner Ward

The main kitchen in the south-west corner of the inner ward. Alongside is a small latrine chamber, originally reached by a flight of steps.

The main kitchen, against the south-west curtain wall, is a remarkably complete medieval example surviving to its full height. It was probably built as part of the late thirteenth- or early fourteenth-century refurbishment of the castle. The kitchen contains a fireplace in each of the gable walls, an oven built into the back of the curtain and various cupboards. Outside the building, on the north, there is a small latrine chamber, lit by a vent in the roof. Built to serve the nearby domestic staff, it was originally reached by a flight of steps. Reference is made to repairing this latrine in 1442–43.

Mention has already been made of a possible forebuilding for the north-west tower (p. 37) and the slit windows in the curtain between the north gate and latrine chamber may have lit such a timber-framed range built against the curtain wall.

Moreover, it is worth remembering that not all the buildings that originally stood in the castle's two wards have survived, especially if they were built of timber. Fifteenth-century documents mention the purchase of a bucket for two pennies for the fountain, a reference presumably to the water supply of the castle. Mention is also made of a granary and hay house, the last named presumably situated close to the stables. The tidying of a garden in the inner ward is also recorded at various times, a feature that has been recognized elsewhere within the confines of castle walls, such as at Conwy.

Further Reading

Acknowledgements

Cadw and the author would like to thank the late Professor Rees Davies and Professor Ralph Griffiths for their assistance with the text, Stephen Priestley, who transcribed the Duchy of Lancaster accounts, and Peter Brears, who studied the kitchens and other domestic arrangements.

Richard Avent, 'The Early Development of Three Coastal Castles', in Heather James, editor, *Sir Gâr: Studies in Carmarthenshire History* (Carmarthen 1991), 167–88.

H. M. Colvin, general editor, *The History of the King's Works*, vol II (London 1963), 685–87.

R. R. Davies, *Conquest, Coexistence and Change: Wales 1063–1415* (Oxford 1987); reprinted in paperback as *The Age of Conquest: Wales 1063–1415* (Oxford 1991).

R. R. Davies, *The Revolt of Owain Glyn Dŵr* (Oxford 1995); reprinted in paperback (Oxford 1997).

Gwynfor Evans, *Gwenllian: Arwres Gymreig/Gwenllian: A Welsh Heroine* (Cardiff 1991).

C. Fox and C. A. R. Radford, 'Kidwelly Castle, Carmarthenshire', *Archaeologia* **83** (1933), 93–138.

R. A. Griffiths, *Sir Rhys ap Thomas and his Family* (Cardiff 1993).

Heather James, 'Topographical Notes on the Early Mediaeval Borough of Kidwelly', *The Carmarthenshire Antiquary* **16** (1980), 6–17.

E. J. Kealey, *Roger of Salisbury, Viceroy of England* (Berkeley, California 1972).

John R. Kenyon, 'Kidwelly Castle, Carmarthenshire: The Reinterpretation of a Monument', in John R. Kenyon and Kieran O'Conor, editors, *The Medieval Castle in Ireland and Wales* (Dublin 2003), 176–81.

Thomas Lloyd, Julian Orbach and Robert Scourfield, *Carmarthenshire and Ceredigion (The Buildings of Wales)* (London 2006).

C. Platt, *The Castle in Medieval England and Wales* (London 1982).

C. A. R. Radford, *Kidwelly Castle*, second edition (London 1952).

R. A. Stalley, 'A Twelfth-Century Patron of Architecture: A Study of the Buildings Erected by Roger, Bishop of Salisbury 1102–1139', *Journal of the British Archaeological Association*, 3rd series, **34** (1971), 62–83.

Roger Turvey, 'The Defences of Twelfth-Century Deheubarth and the Castle Strategy of the Lord Rhys', *Archaeologia Cambrensis* **144** (1995), 103–32.

Roger Turvey, 'Twelve Days That Shook South-West Wales: The Royal Letters, Owain Glyn Dŵr and the Campaign of July 1403', *The Carmarthenshire Antiquary* **37** (2001), 5–20.

Glanmor Williams, *Recovery, Reorientation and Reformation: Wales c. 1415–1642* (Oxford 1987); reprinted in paperback as *Renewal and Reformation: Wales c. 1415–1642* (Oxford 1993).